CH

SPORTS ALL-STARS

MATT RYAN

Jon M. Fishman

Lerner Publications ◆ Minneapolis

Lerner Publications Company
A division of Lerner Publishing Group, Inc.
241 First Avenue North
Minneapolis, MN 55401 USA

For reading levels and more information, look up this title at www.lernerbooks.com.

Library of Congress Cataloging-in-Publication Data

Names: Fishman, Jon M., author.
Title: Matt Ryan / Jon M. Fishman.
Description: Minneapolis : Lerner Publications, 2018. | Series: Sports All-Stars |
    Includes bibliographical references and index. | Audience: Age 7–11. | Audience:
    Grade 4 to 6. | Description based on print version record and CIP data provided by
    publisher; resource not viewed.
Identifiers: LCCN 2017011955 (print) | LCCN 2017015954 (ebook) |
    ISBN 9781512482652 (eb pdf) | ISBN 9781512482492 (lb : alk. paper)
Subjects: LCSH: Ryan, Matt, 1985–—Juvenile literature. | Football players—United
    States—Biography—Juvenile literature. | Quarterbacks (Football)—United
    States—Biography—Juvenile literature.
Classification: LCC GV939.R92 (ebook) | LCC GV939.R92 F57 2018 (print) | DDC
    796.33092 [B]—dc23

LC record available at https://lccn.loc.gov/2017011955

Manufactured in the United States of America
1-43298-33118-9/1/2017

CONTENTS

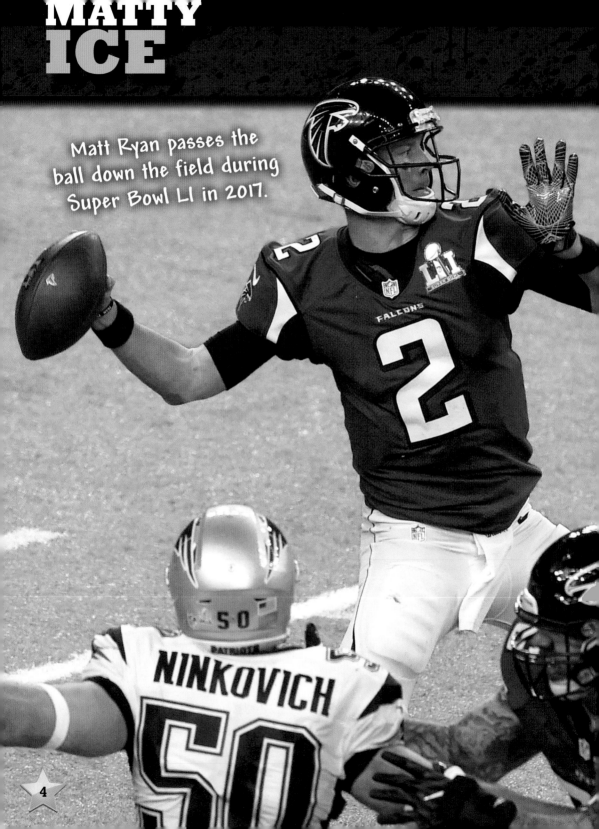

MATTY ICE

Matt Ryan passes the ball down the field during Super Bowl LI in 2017.

Cool. Calm. Steady. Matt Ryan's friends and teammates have used all these words to describe the quarterback when he's on the football field. Some joke that he has ice in his veins instead of blood. Since high school, they've called him Matty Ice.

With millions of fans around the world watching his every move, the Atlanta Falcons quarterback stepped onto the field. It was the second quarter of Super Bowl LI in Houston, Texas. With the score Atlanta 0, New England Patriots 0, the fans were ready for some action. Ryan was about to deliver.

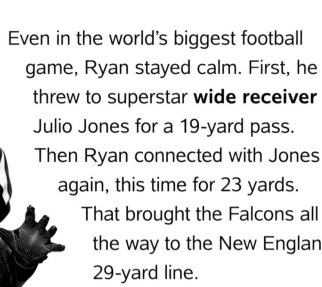

Even in the world's biggest football game, Ryan stayed calm. First, he threw to superstar **wide receiver** Julio Jones for a 19-yard pass. Then Ryan connected with Jones again, this time for 23 yards. That brought the Falcons all the way to the New England 29-yard line.

From there, **running back** Devonta Freeman took over. He pounded through the New England defense for a touchdown. The score was now 7–0, Atlanta.

Ryan was just getting started. When the Falcons took possession of the ball again, he showed everyone why people call him Matty Ice.

Ryan looks for a receiver as he prepares to pass during Super Bowl LI.

He led Atlanta down the field with three long passes. The last pass was a 19-yard touchdown throw to Austin Hooper. It was Falcons 14, Patriots 0!

Austin Hooper runs past a Patriots defender to catch a touchdown pass from Ryan.

Atlanta was on fire. Patriots quarterback Tom Brady and his teammates were desperate to score and get back in the game. Brady heaved a long pass, but it was caught by Atlanta defender Robert Alford. **Interception**! Alford raced 82 yards for a touchdown. The big play made the score 21–0. New England kicked a **field goal** to make it 21–3 at halftime.

In the second half, Ryan led Atlanta 75 yards down the field. A touchdown pass to Tevin Coleman put the Falcons ahead by 25 points. Atlanta seemed unbeatable. After all, no team had ever won a Super Bowl after being behind by more than 10 points.

But then the Patriots started scoring. They made it 28–9, then 28–12. Meanwhile, the New England defense played better against the Falcons. Soon the score was 28–20. Incredibly, the Patriots tied the game with less than a minute left on the game clock. Then they scored in **overtime** to win the Super Bowl.

Ryan and the Falcons were heartbroken. It hurt to have come so close to winning the biggest prize in the National Football League (NFL) only to have it taken away in the end. But Ryan held his head high. He told his fans that he and his teammates would overcome the defeat. And he told them to get ready for an even better season next year.

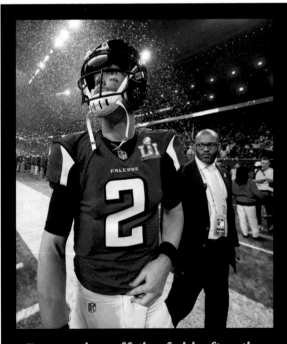

Ryan walks off the field after the Falcons' 34–28 loss to the Patriots.

Ryan plays in a college football game in 2006.

Matt grew up in Exton, Pennsylvania.
He was born there on May 17, 1985. Exton is about 30 miles (48 km) from Philadelphia.

Winning comes naturally to Matt. He's been doing it since eighth grade when he played football for the Philadelphia Little Quakers. Even then, he was

Joe Montana grew up in Pennsylvania. He spent most of his NFL career with the San Francisco 49ers.

cool and calm on the field. Matt knew what the defense was going to do, and he could make quick decisions to change plays during a game.

He was destined to become a football player. His brothers, cousins, and uncles all played the sport. His location also helped. Pennsylvania has a rich football history, especially at the quarterback position. Many all-time great quarterbacks grew up in Pennsylvania, including Dan Marino, Joe Montana, and Johnny Unitas. All three quarterbacks are in the Pro Football Hall of Fame.

Matt attended high school in Philadelphia at William Penn Charter School. By his junior year, he had grown to 6 feet 4 (1.9 m). He had a strong throwing arm, and he could hit his targets with the ball.

Even though they had a future NFL star at quarterback, Penn Charter didn't throw the ball very much. The team used a strategy on offense called the **triple option**. That meant either Matt or one of the running backs usually ran with the ball. The tall quarterback didn't often get a chance to show off his throwing ability. But that was OK with him.

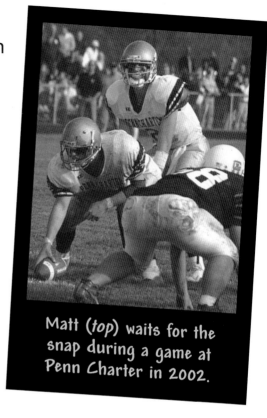

Matt (*top*) waits for the snap during a game at Penn Charter in 2002.

William Penn Charter School has been teaching students since 1689. That makes it one of the oldest schools in the country. William Penn was the founder of Pennsylvania.

Winning games was most important to Matt. "I love to win," he said.

He wasn't a flashy player, but that didn't stop colleges with big-time football teams from noticing him. Coaches at the University of Iowa and Boston College (BC) thought he could be a star. Matt chose BC. The school's football team had an offensive strategy that was similar to the strategies of NFL teams. That meant lots of passing plays. Matt was ready to show the world what he could do.

Ryan played for BC from 2004 to 2007.

Ryan holds the ball during a college game against the University of Notre Dame.

Ryan shows off his new Falcons jersey after being drafted by the team in 2008.

As a senior in 2007, he threw an incredible 31 touchdown passes in just 14 games. He was named the player of the year in his **conference**. He also won the Manning Award as the most outstanding quarterback in college football.

In April 2008, the Falcons chose Ryan with the third pick in the NFL **draft**. He couldn't wait to get his NFL career started. "I wanted to be a Falcon," he said. "I'm so excited to be going down there."

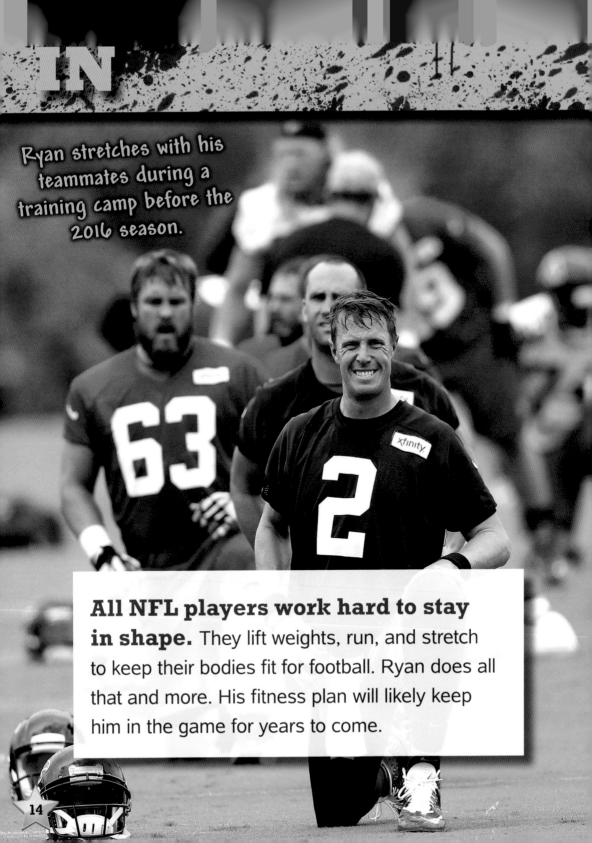

Ryan stretches with his teammates during a training camp before the 2016 season.

All NFL players work hard to stay in shape. They lift weights, run, and stretch to keep their bodies fit for football. Ryan does all that and more. His fitness plan will likely keep him in the game for years to come.

Ryan practices passing during an NFL training camp.

He ran and worked out in high school. But he admits that he didn't think too much about why he was doing it. In college, trainers helped him understand how exercise could make him a better football player. He'd be able to throw the ball farther, and he wouldn't be as tired near the end of games. Once Ryan understood that, he was all-in.

To get ready for the NFL, Ryan worked on specific skills he knew were important in the league. He ran the 40-yard dash over and over again until he could do it faster than he ever had before. He practiced drills such as the **vertical jump**. Ryan knew that running and jumping skills would help him stay away from defenders on the field.

After he'd been in the league a few years, Ryan began to look for new ways to strengthen his body. He worked with trainers to create exercises that would help him throw farther than ever. One drill had him rapidly swinging a baseball bat to strengthen his muscles. In another, Ryan threw

The Atlanta Falcons warm up in a practice before the Super Bowl in 2017.

footballs while on his knees. He worked at it until he could throw almost as far from his knees as he could from his feet!

Quarterbacks must keep track of dozens of plays and remember them quickly in stressful situations. They're also expected to be team leaders on the field. Ryan knows that mental strength is just as important as physical strength. He works with trainers to strengthen his confidence. All people make mistakes and fail sometimes. Ryan prepares his mind to deal with these failures and learn from them.

Diet is an important part of Ryan's fitness. He eats lots of vegetables and fish. He makes his meals colorful so he's sure to be eating many different foods. Of course, sometimes he cheats on his diet with cheesy pizza or vanilla ice cream.

In 2016, Ryan and his teammates got a big surprise. Their coach arranged for them to train with a group of US Navy SEALs. SEALs are some of the toughest and best-trained soldiers in the US military.

For four days, the SEALs put the Falcons through exercises that focused on teamwork. They did push-ups together while counting out loud as the SEALs tried to rattle them with loud noises. Teams of six players carried 240-pound (109 kg) logs until they were told they could drop them. The workouts had a big impact on Ryan. "The bravery that [the SEALs] have and their discipline and attention to detail, to me it was eye opening," he said.

A group of Navy SEALs works together to carry a log. SEALs complete intense physical and mental training to prepare for military missions.

19

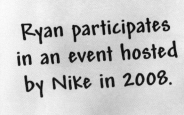

Ryan participates in an event hosted by Nike in 2008.

Matt Ryan loves football. If he had another job, he would probably play football for fun. Luckily for him, he gets paid a lot to play the sport he loves. In 2013, he began a new **contract** with the Falcons. They agreed to pay him $103,750,000 over the next five years! That made him the NFL's second-highest-paid player at the time.

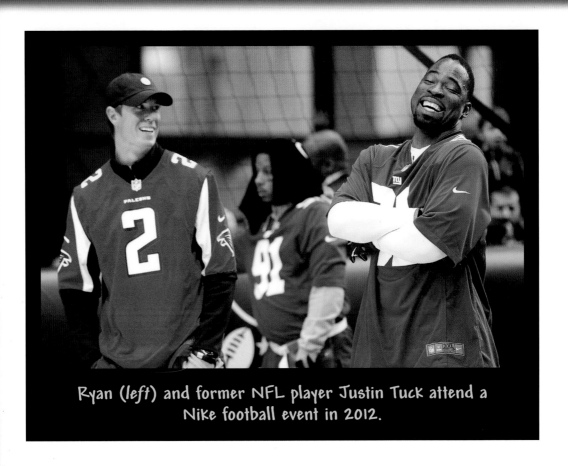

Ryan (*left*) and former NFL player Justin Tuck attend a Nike football event in 2012.

Money from the NFL is only the beginning of Ryan's earnings. He also gets paid to promote products. He has deals with companies such as Nike and Comcast to be in magazine and TV ads. He appears in lots of commercials, such as a funny ad for ESPN that pokes fun at the many plays a quarterback has to remember.

Finding Sarah Marshall

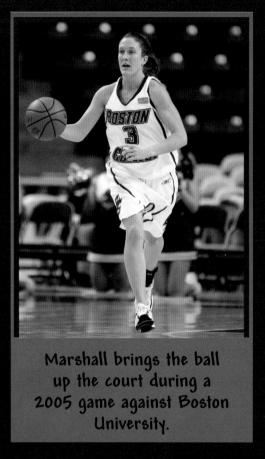

Marshall brings the ball up the court during a 2005 game against Boston University.

Lifting weights in college helped Ryan become a superstar quarterback. It also helped him find a wife! He met Sarah Marshall in the weight room at Boston College when they were both freshmen. The couple got married in 2011.

Matt Ryan is the famous athlete in the family, but Sarah Ryan is no slouch when it comes to sports. She played **point guard** on the Boston College basketball team. She graduated as one of the team's all-time great passers. Since then, she has stayed off the court. "Finding a parking spot at [the grocery store] on a Sunday continues to be the most competitive thing I've done since playing college basketball," she joked on Twitter.

Ryan makes good use of his money by giving back to his community. Each year, he pays for the Little Quakers team in Atlanta to attend a Falcons game. He also buys the whole team special jerseys.

In 2014, Matt and his wife, Sarah, gave away $125,000. The money is used to provide scholarships for students at her former high school. Scholarships are awarded to students in need who show strong leadership skills.

Ryan celebrates a 2017 win with his wife.

MATT RYAN, SUPERSTAR

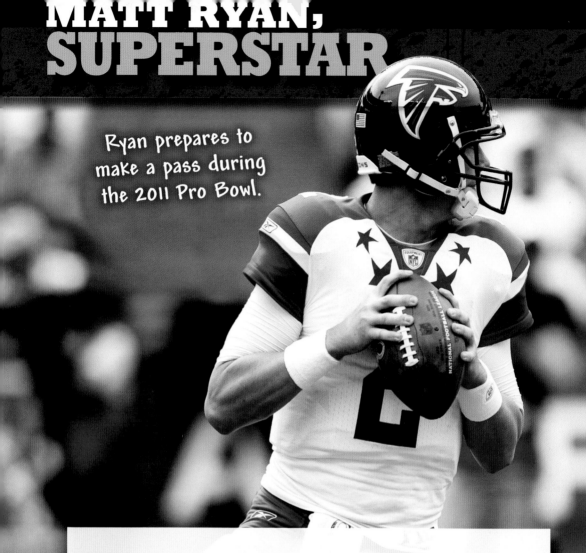

Ryan prepares to make a pass during the 2011 Pro Bowl.

Ryan has been considered one of the world's best quarterbacks since his first year in the NFL. He threw 16 touchdown passes that season and was named Offensive Rookie of the Year. He improved his touchdown totals in each of the next four seasons. Eight times

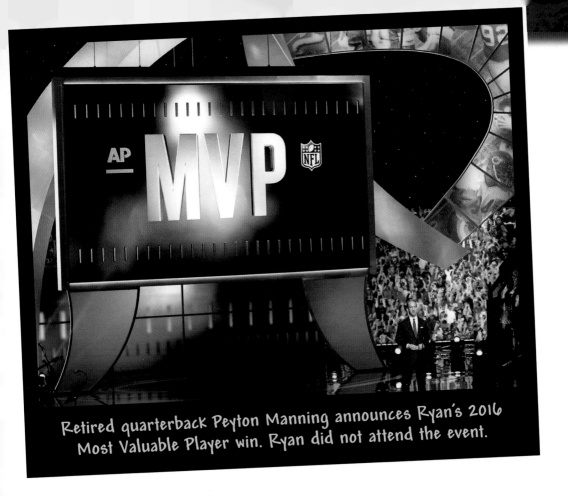

Retired quarterback Peyton Manning announces Ryan's 2016 Most Valuable Player win. Ryan did not attend the event.

he has been the NFL Player of the Week, and he's been voted to the **Pro Bowl** four times.

It wasn't until 2016, though, that Ryan truly became a superstar. That year he threw an incredible 38 touchdown passes with only seven interceptions. Those hard-to-believe numbers helped him win the NFL Most Valuable

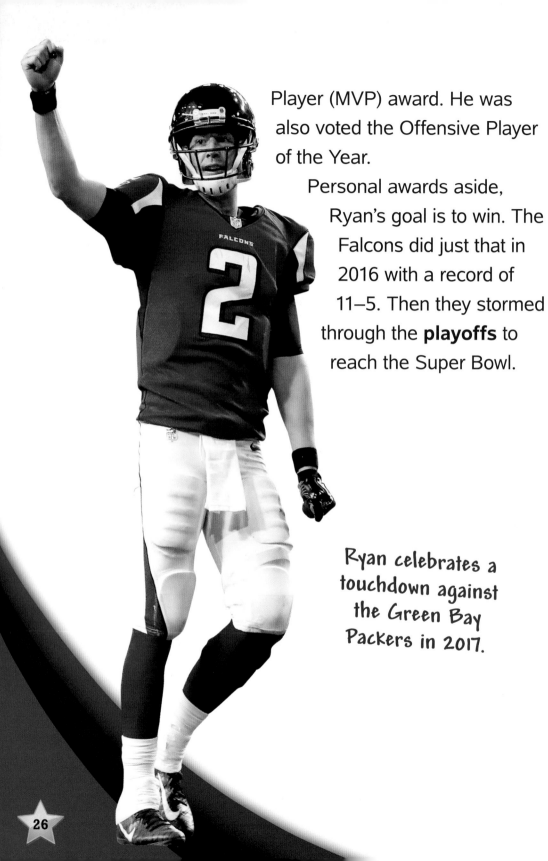

Player (MVP) award. He was also voted the Offensive Player of the Year.

Personal awards aside, Ryan's goal is to win. The Falcons did just that in 2016 with a record of 11–5. Then they stormed through the **playoffs** to reach the Super Bowl.

Ryan celebrates a touchdown against the Green Bay Packers in 2017.

Ryan speaks at a press conference after losing to the Patriots in the Super Bowl.

Losing to the Patriots in the big game was hard for the Atlanta players and fans. Ryan was crushed, and he thought about what he could have done differently in the game. But he knows everyone has setbacks, and he knows how to handle them. Soon Ryan felt like himself again. "I'm pretty simple to understand," he said. "I want to win."

All-Star Stats

Matt Ryan is the Falcons' all-time leader in touchdown passes. But his most impressive stat may be passing yards. He's already 21st on the list of NFL all-time passing yards leaders. For Atlanta, he's alone in first place, and no one else is even close.

Most Passing Yards in Atlanta Falcons History

Player	Passing Yards
Matt Ryan	37,701
Steve Bartkowski	23,470
Chris Miller	14,066
Chris Chandler	13,268
Michael Vick	11,505
Jeff George	8,575
Bob Berry	8,489
Bobby Hebert	7,053
Randy Johnson	5,538
David Archer	4,275

Source Notes

12 Jenny Vrentas, "Matt Ryan Is Old School," *Sports Illustrated*, January 24, 2017, http://mmqb.si.com /mmqb/2017/01/24/matt-ryan-falcons-philadelphia-penn -charter-school.

13 Bob Ryan, "Ryan Pick Should Fly," *Boston.com*, April 27, 2008, http://archive.boston.com/sports/articles/2008/04/27 /ryan_pick_should_fly.

18 Kalyn Kahler, "When Falcons Train with SEALs," *Sports Illustrated*, May 11, 2016, http://mmqb.si.com /mmqb/2016/05/11/atlanta-falcons-nfl-training-navy-seals -dan-quinn-matt-ryan.

22 Taylor Vortherms, "Sarah Ryan, Wife of the Falcons' QB, Touches Lives in Maine, Georgia," *Portland (ME) Press Herald*, February 5, 2017, http://www.pressherald .com/2017/02/05/sarah-ryan-wife-of-the-falcons-qb -touches-lives-in-maine-georgia/.

27 Joseph Santoliquito, "Maxwell Club to Honor Matt Ryan as Bert Bell Winner," *CBS Philly*, March 7, 2017, http://philadelphia.cbslocal.com/2017/03/07/maxwell-club -matt-ryan-bert-bell/.

Glossary

conference: a group of teams that play against one another

contract: an agreement between a player and a team that states how much the player will be paid and for how long

draft: an event in which teams take turns choosing new players

field goal: a kick that goes between the poles at the ends of a football field. A field goal is worth three points.

interception: a pass caught by the opposing team that results in the ball changing possession

overtime: an extra period of play in a game

playoffs: a series of games held each season to decide a champion

point guard: a basketball player who leads a team when they have the ball

Pro Bowl: a game held each season to celebrate the NFL's best players

running back: a player whose main job is to run with the ball

triple option: an offensive strategy that usually results in one of three players running the ball

vertical jump: a jump straight up in the air from a standing position

wide receiver: a player whose main job is to catch passes

30

Further Information

Atlanta Falcons
http://www.atlantafalcons.com

Braun, Eric. *Tom Brady*. Minneapolis: Lerner Publications, 2017.

Football Facts
https://kidskonnect.com/sports/football

Mack, Larry. *The Atlanta Falcons Story*. Minneapolis: Bellwether Media, 2017.

NFL Rush
http://www.nflrush.com

Savage, Jeff. *Football Super Stats*. Minneapolis: Lerner Publications, 2018.

Index

Photo Acknowledgments

The images in this book are used with the permission of: iStock.com/63151 (gold and silver stars); ZUMA Press, Inc./Alamy Stock Photo, p. 2; Focus on Sport/ Getty Images, pp. 4–5, 6, 7; Tom Pennington/Getty Images, pp. 8, 26; Jim Rogash/ WireImage/Getty Images, p. 9; Peter Brouillet/Getty Images, p. 10; Courtesy of William Penn Charter School, p. 11; Andy Altenburger/Icon SMI/Getty Images, p. 12; Chris Szagola/Cal Sport Media/Newscom, p. 13; AP Photo/John Bazemore, pp. 14, 15; Tim Warner/Getty Images, pp. 16–17; Richard Schoenberg/Corbis/Getty Images, p. 19; Robert Sabo/NY Daily News Archive/Getty Images, p. 20; Andrew H. Walker/ Getty Images, p. 21; Robert E. Klein/Icon SMI/Newscom, p. 22; Kevin C. Cox/Getty Images, p. 23; AP Photo/Jim Mahoney, p. 24; Bob Levey/Getty Images, p. 25; Larry Busacca/Getty Images, p. 27.

Front cover: ZUMA Press, Inc./Alamy Stock Photo; iStock.com/neyro2008.